AF602017

IT'S YOUR TIME TO RISE

120 Motivational Notes To Empower You On Your Journey to Transforming Your Life.

VENISE D. ALLEN

This book is intended for empowerment and motivational purposes only.

It's Your Time To Rise: *120 Motivational Notes to Empower You on Your Journey to Transforming Your Life.*

Distributed by VP 35 Plus LLC
Miami, FL

For permission requests, ordering information, and bulk purchases, please write to the publisher at the email address below.

Email: vp35pluspub@gmail.com

May your intentions be more potent than the criticism from your critics.

TABLE OF CONTENTS

INTRODUCTION

Are you going through a transformational phase or about to embark on your journey towards change? Congratulations! You have surrendered to a trip that will forever impact and influence your life and the lives of those around you.

In the coming pages, you will receive motivational notes affirming, encouraging, and strengthening as you courageously rise and embark on the journey to transform your life. These notes were whispers of encouragement and instructions I received in my spirit while going through my transformational process. They are kind words that have motivated and grounded me in myself, my faith in God, and my journey. By sharing them with you, I aim to strengthen and encourage you as you pursue your transformational journey.

Transformation is long. It is often lonely and complex, and most people journey alone. The transformation process sometimes feels hopeless and makes you question your sense of self and desire for change. The pain and discomfort that transformation causes will make you want to revert to your old self and habits because advancing seems riskier than remaining the same or going backward.

One thing about change is that it is challenging; however, the cost of not pursuing change is far more detrimental. So, don't shy away from the challenges; instead, embrace them by focusing on the feeling of achieving your desired goal and what it will do for you. Let the coming pages guide you to your success. The more you encourage yourself to persevere, the more enthralled you will become by the experience, and the more you will appreciate the lessons you learn along the journey. So, here's to your courage to rise!

SECTION ONE:
FAITH BOOSTERS

HEBREWS 11:1-3 ESV

Now faith is the assurance of things hoped for, the conviction of things not seen. For by it, the people of old received their commendation. By faith, we understand that the universe was created by the word of God so that what is seen was not made out of things that are visible.

GALATIANS 5:16 ESV

But I say, walk by the Spirit, and you will not gratify the desires of the flesh.

MATTHEW 22:21 ESV

And whatever you ask in prayer, you will receive if you have faith.

1

Godly guidance does not need to make sense to the human mind/rationale to be followed.

2

If you feel at peace with your decision, do it.

3

Take action. The longer you stay "on the fence" about making decisions, the more you punish yourself. So choose one side, leap over to it, and pick yourself up afterward.

4

Fear will keep you running around in circles; you will always arrive at the same destination even if your route seems different. Therefore, face the fear and take the risk; at least you'll end up at a new destination, and you can start from there.

5

Fear is real, but so is God who calls us to have faith. Therefore, keep moving until God settles and establishes you.

6

The Glory of the Lord is your rear guard. Go forward in faith.

7

The task only seems impossible until you get it done.

8

Taking risks is more beneficial than staying in your comfort zone.

9

Some moments are not for a lifetime. Sometimes you only get one shot; you cannot afford to miss it.

10

Have the courage to grow into the unknown.

11

If God is calling you to give up everything (whatever it is you hold dear), be willing and courageous enough to let it go. God is the greatest giver and will give you more than you have to relinquish.

12

The moment you decide to grow and prosper is when the journey gets tough. Every level requires more effort, but persevere, for your rewards will be great.

13

God is very strategic. He will control nature and influence strangers to help, protect and provide for the fulfillment of His purpose through you.

14

God knows where you are going and the best route to get you there. Trust His guidance.

15

Don't be discouraged. Experiencing doubt is normal. Remain strong and hold on to your vision.

16

Things have a way of working out. No matter how impossible it seems. Just stand still, trust God, and watch Him make a way.

17

Disruptions in your life should not be considered enemy attacks. Instead, disruptions should be viewed as the birthplace of something new and extraordinary.

18

Prepare for everything you desire, even when you are not sure how the opportunity will manifest.

19

Be the reason someone develops the courage to save themselves.

20

Stand in power. Keep doing good. Remember your creator.

SECTION TWO:
SELF-AFFIRMATIONS

DEUTERONOMY 31:8 ESV

It is the LORD who goes before you. He will be with you. He will not leave you or forsake you. Do not fear or be dismayed."

1 PETER 2:9 ESV

But you are a chosen race, a royal priesthood, a holy nation, a people for his own possession, that you may proclaim the excellencies of him who called you out of darkness into his marvelous light.

PHILIPPIANS 4:13 ESV

I can do all things through him who strengthens me.

21

You are brave. You are loved. You are strong.
You matter.

22

To be unstoppable, you must believe in yourself.

23

Your life requires balance to be who you
intrinsically are.

24

Take a moment to celebrate where you are in life. It is either a product of your growth or a place that will help you to grow.

25

God's best is always inside of you and before you. Don't get stuck on the past or what is happening now. Learn the lessons and keep moving forward.

26

Rejoice and be glad. Today is new, and it is filled with so many blessings.

27

Be strong in the face of adversity. You are capable of overcoming challenges.

28

You deserve to see and experience yourself in the same light as you see others.

29

You may not be recognized for your progression now, but if you believe in yourself enough, believe in what you do, and be consistent, you will most definitely be rewarded.

30

Miracles can happen just by the snap of a finger, and other times it takes a little longer. Just know that waiting on a miracle is better than settling.

31

Circumstances all around will cause you to question your goals, plans, dreams, and desires. Sometimes you may even want to quit and start a different and less strategic plan, set less ambitious goals, or even deny the dreams you have. However, remember that these dreams were placed in your heart for a reason. You've got what it takes! So rest if you desire, but never doubt or give up on yourself.

32

Being you, your most authentic you, is magical.

33

There is something extraordinary in every experience, and greatness is everywhere.

34

You are the most important manifestation of God. With the authority you were given upon entering this world, you can create beauty from unpleasant situations.

35

Trust your intuition. Trust your heart. Trust the voice of the divine Holy Spirit that lives within you.

36

Be grateful for the little things while you wait for the big things to fall into place.

37

Your happiness is founded in Jesus Christ. It is yours now and for all eternity.

38

I promise you this one thing; one day, you will look back and be so grateful for the things that did not work out how you thought you wanted them to. Trust the process. All things work together for your good.

39

Life does not have to be perfect to be beautiful. Nothing needs to be perfect. Find beauty in the imperfections, be grateful, and just vibe.

40

Your good precedes you. It gets to destinations before you do. You have ears, and you can hear. You have eyes, and you can see. Be alert to your intuition and your good shall not escape you.

SECTION THREE:
MENTAL HEALTH AND WELL-BEING

1 PETER 5:10 ESV

And after you have suffered a little while, the God of all grace, who has called you to his eternal glory in Christ, will himself restore, confirm, strengthen, and establish you.

1 JOHN 4:18 ESV

There is no fear in love. But perfect love drives out fear because fear has to do with punishment. The one who fears is not made perfect in love.

PSALMS 23:1-4 ESV

The LORD is my shepherd; I shall not want. He makes me lie down in green pastures. He leads me beside still waters. He restores my soul. He leads me in paths of righteousness for his name's sake. Even though I walk through the valley of the shadow of death, I will fear no evil, for you are with me; your rod and your staff comfort me.

41

Invest in your healing. Healing helps you accept yourself and present your most authentic self in every area of your life.

42

Be genuinely vulnerable. Know and accept that you are not perfect. But know that God loves you anyway.

43

Your self-esteem is personal and should only bear meaning to you, therefore, spend your time doing worthwhile things to make you feel better about yourself.

44

Fear can legitimately protect you. Fear can legitimately trap you. Learn to discern the difference.

45

Control less; trust God more. The more you fight to achieve an outcome, the more it becomes elusive.

46

Trying to escape your problems is like running away from yourself. There is no escape when your issue is always within you.

47

Seasons change. Situations change. Nothing remains the same over time. Take this knowledge and make every experience an adventure so that you can relish the moments as they come.

48

To fully experience life, you must engage with your eyes wide open. Let yourself feel all the feelings, then free yourself to fully and appropriately express how you feel.

49

When you are kind to yourself, you will understand the need to be kind to others. In addition, being kind to others helps you to believe in yourself more.

50

Positivity gets you on the brighter side of life. On the brighter side of life, things are always more straightforward.

51

Growing up means taking responsibility for your life and your destiny.

52

Every individual is affected by fear. The difference is that great people are relentless regardless of fear's existence.

53

Never be afraid to redefine your journey. It is always good to do right by others, but your first and most crucial responsibility is to yourself.

54

Focus on the things and people that matter. Everything else and everyone else is a distraction.

55

Your identity is not defined by your possessions, positions, pain, comfort zones, children, or spouse. Instead, your identity is defined by your connection to your creator.

56

Being joyful keeps you attuned to blissful moments. So have an open mind and tune into the things that bring you joy.

57

Love what you have, and you will realize that you have everything you need. Start with yourself and love yourself first.

58

There is tremendous joy in valuing and appreciating the simplicity that surrounds you.

59

Your number one priority is your peace and total alignment. This ultimately creates happiness in and around you. Therefore, practice choosing what is best for you without feeling guilty about it.

60

Joy is found in feeding your soul, not your ego. So make the time to do something each day that is good for your soul.

SECTION FOUR:
PERSONAL GROWTH

PHILIPPIANS 1:6 ESV

And I am sure of this one thing, that He who began a good work in you will bring it to completion at the day of Jesus Christ.

ROMANS 8:28 ESV

And we know that for those who love God, all things work together for good, for those who are called according to his purpose.

3 JOHN 1:2 ESV

Beloved, I pray that all may go well with you and that you may be in good health, as it goes well with your soul.

61

Like a tree, your growth is between you and God. Your painful experience represents the dirt. What you pour into your soul to feel better and acquire knowledge represents water, and the sun represents Jesus Christ—the Son of God. Let this understanding encourage you as you grow into the person you desire to become.

62

Nature possesses the two most powerful tools for success. They are organization and time. Once you have an idea of what you intrinsically desire, organize yourself by preparing and doing what is required to achieve it. As you prepare, wait. Wait for the right time. Finally, the time will come, and you must present what you have prepared.

63

Working on yourself includes making more money, a better education, a job, a home, and more; however, the most significant work you can do on yourself is to cleanse your soul, forgive, express gratitude, and cultivate your intangible characteristics.

64

Regardless of your challenges, you should continuously pursue expansion. When you grow, you inspire others.

65

If you continue to stick around, accept, fight for, or settle for crumbs, you will never know the value of eating from a full bowl.

66

Your cup being half-full or half-empty is irrelevant. What's important, however, is that you have a cup, and something is in it. That is potential right there!

67

A significant sign of growth is detaching yourself from the material world and pursuing a more transcendent existence. Minimalism is a lifestyle that rewards you greatly.

68

Only a few of your experiences will be good, but every experience will teach you something valuable. Therefore, focus on the lesson, for it will cause you to align with God's will for your life.

69

When you own your story, opportunities open for you to change your life. It is your journey, own it and live it for you.

70

Your capacity to allow people to live their truth different from yours without losing compassion for them is a true reflection of how powerful your love is.

71

Self-discipline is self-love. Self-love is self-discipline. One cannot exist without the other.

72

Happiness cannot be acquired and stored for when needed or wanted. Happiness is an energy that flows from within yourself when you forgive, express gratitude, and love others as you love yourself.

73

Knowledge can never be enough when living in an ever-advancing world.

74

No matter how you fail or how often you fail, there is always an opportunity amid the failure for growth.

75

You can appreciate the light but must know the darkness before that.

76

Exposure to alternatives is sometimes necessary because it helps you figure out what you want to do with your life.

77

Create space for growth in every area of your life. Growth is necessary to help you remain relevant in an ever-advancing society.

78

You can change anything about yourself if you so desire. All you must do is decide, create, and act. Then rehearse it until it becomes a habit.

79

Dwelling on negativity is a form of self-sabotage. You win by only being positive and acknowledging the positive perspectives.

80

You are made to persist. That's how you find the meaning of your life and grow into who you are.

SECTION FIVE:
SELF-DEVELOPMENT

1 PETER 5:6-7 ESV

Humble yourself, therefore, under the mighty hand of God so that at the proper time, He may exalt you, casting all your anxieties on Him because He cares for you.

1 THESSALONIANS 5:11 ESV

Therefore encourage one another and build one another up, just as you are doing.

ROMANS 5:13 ESV

May the God of hope fill you with all joy and peace as you trust in him so that you may overflow with hope by the power of the Holy Spirit.

81

Identify the things that you are good at. Perfect them with additional training, then put all your effort into doing them.

82

Work with what you have until you can put what you have to work for you.

83

Speak power, positivity, health, money, resources, and resourceful people into your life. To live or to die is in the power of your declarations.

84

If whatever you desire doesn't cost you
some sacrifice, it won't benefit you.

85

When you shut out the noise and trust your gut,
your journey gets much clearer.

86

Become the person you decide to be.
Your soul is rooting for you.

87

If not cultivated, your talents, skills, and knowledge will be useless to you and everyone else.

88

Determination forges pathways.
Relentlessness causes shifts.

89

Don't be afraid to downgrade your current life to make way for a better comeback.

90

Know your "why" (why you do what you do). Your "why" is the foundation for rest, evaluation, recalibration, and success.

91

Decide that you will start, reorganize, or finish your goals today. Your light and destiny depend on it.

92

Be intentional about what you desire. Be free to give your all with the audacious hope of what could be.

93

Your God-given talents are crucial for success. By harnessing those talents, you gain a deeper understanding of your value and, ultimately, discover your authentic purpose.

94

Your visions are waiting to become your reality. Be in love with the idea of their creation and manifestation.

95

May you never be comfortable staying the same every day, but instead choose to grow into the best version of yourself.

96

To have an accurate sense of yourself as you live, you must make conscious choices.

97

The progress you desire requires more courage. So don't be afraid to step up.

98

People will do better than you in every sphere of life. That's not your business. The question is, *are you doing better than you were yesterday?*

99

Don't let life's hardships, failures, hurts, sorrows, and demands take your true self away. Instead, find a magical sweet spot occasionally to connect with yourself.

100

Victory is not promised to those who are strong and capable. Instead, victory is promised to those who, with a growth mindset, endure to the end.

SECTION SIX:
RELATIONSHIPS

HEBREWS 12:1 ESV

Therefore, since we are surrounded by so great a cloud of witnesses, let us also lay aside every weight and sin which clings so closely, and let us run with endurance the race set before us.

MATTHEW 19:26 ESV

But Jesus looked at them and said, "With man, this is impossible, but with God, all things are possible."

JAMES 2:18 ESV

But someone will say, "You have faith, and I have works," Show me your faith apart from your works, and I will show you my faith by my works."

101

There is someone out there for you. You do not have to settle. Instead, focus on being your best, most valuable, and authentic self. After all, those are the qualities that your person is looking for in you.

102

Self-control is a powerful skill. Once you can control yourself, you can handle any situation.

103

You will never overcome the obstacles you choose to avoid. Victory can only be obtained you face them.

104

Enjoy all your weirdness and quirks.
They add to the attributes that will attract the right people to you.

105

Never let anyone get comfortable treating you less than you deserve. Their happiness and satisfaction should not come at your expense.

106

You are the most important person in your life. Invest in yourself, treat yourself, care for yourself, and love yourself.

107

Never lowball yourself. You are worth way more than you believe.

108

Rejection is normal. Learn to accept it as much as you give it. It is not the end of your life. Instead, it either saves you or creates opportunities for you.

109

Don't create a single reason to stay in a situation that gives you one hundred reasons to leave.

110

Values, like the foundation of a building, are the foundations of a healthy life and lifestyle. Therefore, the values you identify and establish, or the lack thereof, are significant determinants of your relationships and future outcomes.

111

You are valuable, and value is what you should endeavor to give. Giving value expresses who you are and what makes you feel satisfied. Giving value is never about the other person; giving value is about you.

112

Rationalize your feelings. Your intuition may very well be teaching you something.

113

Don't compare yourself and your journey to anyone else's. Never criticize another individual's lifestyle and choices to make yourself feel superior. It never benefits you.

114

Someone's behavior towards you tells you two things—how they feel about you and their emotional maturity. It's not personal, but make a note and proceed accordingly.

115

Learn. Learn. Learn. There is something to be learned in every situation. Your interactions act as a mirror that reflects how you are showing up to others.

116

Let people be who they are for themselves.
You become who you need to be for yourself.
Don't take things personally.
Your mental health and well-being matter more.

117

Never try to change anyone. Instead, choose to grow and evolve. They will either grow with you or fall away from your life.

118

A relaxed and rejuvenated mind and body can significantly enhance your aura.

119

A positive perspective precedes success.

120

If it happens, it happens. If not, whatever will be, will be. Life is a beautiful adventure regardless. Enjoy the ride.

FINAL THOUGHTS

Nothing about desiring change is easy. Life itself is hard. Your hardships may break you but are not meant to ruin you. With the proper perspective, you will see that they are intended to build your character, integrity, and personality. It is my desire that you find the courage to continuously crave change, purpose, impact, and influence more than your fear of remaining the same. Have the courage to rise, transform your life, and allow the experiences to strengthen, shape, mature, and advance you for your benefit and the good of all.

I am rooting for you!
-Venise.

If this book has been a blessing, we would love to hear about it.

Please send your comments to our publishers at

vp35pluspub@gmail.com.

www.ingramcontent.com/pod-product-compliance
Ingram Content Group UK Ltd.
Pitfield, Milton Keynes, MK11 3LW, UK
UKHW060110300726
14090UKWH00002B/112

* 9 7 9 8 8 9 1 8 4 2 4 0 3 *